CAUSES
OF THE AMERICAN
REVOLUTION

by Randi Reisfeld and Jackie Robb

Table of Contents

6

What were the social, political, economic, and ideological factors that set the stage for America's uprising?

18

The first shots of the American Revolution were fired on
April 19, 1775, at the Battles of Lexington and Concord when
British troops were sent to destroy arms that were being
stored by the colonial militia on a farm outside Boston.

Introduction

Down with Tyranny!

▲ **King George III in 1775**

Early on the morning of April 19, 1775, when the first shot was fired at the Battle of Lexington, Massachusetts, King George III was at home in London. When news of the colonists' uprising finally reached him some weeks later, the king was outraged. The results of his ill-received policies in the American colonies were finally upon him.

King George III had been the ruling monarch of England since 1760 (and would remain on the throne until 1820—one of the longest reigns in British history). As the supreme ruler, he had control not only of his own country and its holdings in Europe, but also of every colony ruled by England around the globe, including those in the Americas. He had come to power during the French and Indian War and emerged victorious in 1763, gaining an empire in North America. But even with the outcome of victory, waging war was not cheap. In order to repay the crown's debt, which had nearly doubled during wartime, the king began enforcing existing laws and imposing duties and tariffs on the colonies. The result was years rife with conflict. King George did not approve of the many thousands of his subjects in the American colonies who refused to pay the taxes. After all, these taxes were levied in order to pay for their defense and well-being. The king was not sympathetic to the colonists' discontent or their underlying desire for change. Now there was mutiny. How had it come to this?

PRIMARY SOURCE

Declaration of Rights and Grievances, 1774

After King George imposed the Intolerable Acts, the First Continental Congress met in Philadelphia and sent a Declaration of Rights and Grievances in 1774 in hopes of a peaceful resolution. You can read the original document online at the Library of Congress website, www.loc.gov.

Social and Political Causes of the Revolution

Who were the colonists, and what social and political factors paved their road to independence?

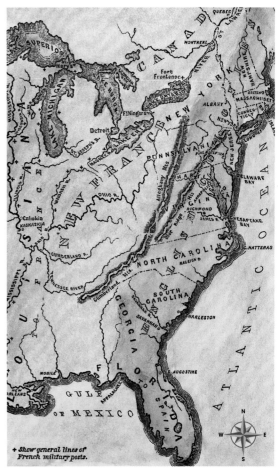

▲ New Hampshire, Massachusetts, Rhode Island, Connecticut, New York, New Jersey, Pennsylvania, Delaware, Maryland, Virginia, North Carolina, South Carolina, and Georgia made up the thirteen original colonies.

The people who rose up against the British crown in 1775 were an eclectic group, some of whom descended from the European settlers who came to North America in the early 1600s and others born in Europe, who followed later. Beginning with the charter for the Virginia colony in 1606, England issued several royal colonial charters granting companies and other groups the right to settle lands in North America. These early settlements established their own colonial governments with varying degrees of success. In addition to having separate governments, these early settlements often were founded by very different groups, with different social, economic, and political goals and ideas.

Governing the Colonies

All of the British colonies were subject to the rule of Great Britain, which was a constitutional **monarchy** in which the king ruled with the help of a representative assembly (British Parliament). However, the colonies were 3,000 miles away from England and by default they largely governed themselves. The colonies that offered both economic opportunity and just laws of self-governance were most effective in attracting future settlers throughout the 1600s and 1700s.

The House of Burgesses

The Jamestown settlement in Virginia was on almost all counts a failure until serious changes were made in order to attract new colonists. One of those reforms was installing a more just government. In 1619, Virginia established its House of Burgesses, the first representative assembly in the colonies, with legislators that were elected by the people. At that time the only people who could vote were land-owning males aged seventeen or older. Though the governor of the colony still retained much control, the House of Burgesses offered the Virginia colonists a role in their own government. The French, Spanish, and Dutch colonies of the era did not have such legislatures.

The Mayflower Compact

In 1620, the *Mayflower* sailed from England headed for "northern Virginia," which at the time extended all the way to what is now New York. The ship was hoping to land at the mouth of the Hudson River, but it blew off course. It landed instead on the shores of what came to be called Plymouth, Massachusetts. Many of the 102 men, women, and children aboard were fleeing from religious **persecution**. These "Separatists," today referred to as **Pilgrims**, were members of a religious order whose beliefs did not always fall in line with the teachings of the Church of England. Citizens who did not follow its teachings risked punishment and even torture. By 1620, when the *Mayflower* sailed away from England, the Pilgrims aboard dreamed of finding a new home where they would have the freedom to worship as they wished. When the people aboard realized they would be settling in unchartered territory, they established the Mayflower Compact, the first written framework of government in the British colonies that outlined the commitment of the people to self-rule.

▲ The intended course of the *Mayflower* would have taken the ship to what is now New York Harbor, but, off by just a few degrees, the ship landed in what is now Cape Cod, Massachusetts.

PRIMARY SOURCE

The original Mayflower Compact is believed to be lost. However, a copy of it appears in Plymouth governor William Bradford's handwritten history *Of Plymouth Plantation*, around 1630.

THEN AND NOW

The Town Meeting

The first town meeting was held by the Puritans in Massachusetts in 1633. Town meetings are still considered one of the purest forms of democracy. When a decision had to be made in the village, the leaders would call a town meeting. Though at first only men could attend and only freemen could vote, over time this forum became a place where every member of the community could voice his or her opinion. Through these meetings, the Puritans helped establish democratic ideals within their colonial culture.

▲ A town meeting is a democratic forum that originated in New England. To this day, town meetings are still held in many states.

Growth and Expansion

New Seekers of Tolerance

Ironically, the Pilgrims and later the Puritans, who fled religious persecution in search of religious **tolerance** within the Church of England, did not always treat others in kind. In fact, they established strict **theocracies** in the colonies. These colonial governments, where the church and clergy governed the people, proved in many cases to be highly intolerant of new ideas and other beliefs. Conflicts over religion were a major social issue in the colonies. When people with differing opinions did not adhere to their religious teachings, they risked **banishment**.

Many who were cast off into exile in the wilderness and excluded from the colony perished of starvation or were killed by Native Americans. Others had enough resolve (and resources and supporters) to start their own colonies elsewhere. This led to new colonies such as Providence Plantation, started by Roger Williams.

Williams, a **theologian**, or religious scholar, who believed in tolerance, started the colony as a place of refuge for religious minorities. He also believed in treating Native Americans with fairness and respect and was one of the first to try to abolish slavery. Anne Hutchinson was another great theologian and leader who disagreed with the Puritan clergy. She settled Portsmouth, Rhode Island, after she was banished from the Massachusetts Bay Colony.

{ **The Root of the Meaning:**
theocracy
}
comes from the Greek word *theokratia*, which means "rule of god."

Pennsylvania, founded by William Penn in 1681, was yet another example of the many experiments in government and society that were occurring in the colonies. Penn started his colony with the intent of forming the first truly free and peaceful society. He wrote the First Frame of Government in order to clearly outline the rights of Pennsylvania colonists. The document secured the right to private property, freedom of enterprise, freedom of the press, religious tolerance, and a right to a trial by jury. It also outlined a two-house legislature with a council that represented the people and a general assembly to approve laws that would be located on-site in Pennsylvania, not England. The council consisted of owners of large amounts of land and could propose laws and appoint officials. The general assembly consisted of medium landowners and could accept or reject legislation coming from the council. As proprietor of Pennsylvania, Penn had veto power over laws passed by the legislature.

New Seekers of Opportunity

While many settlers came to America for religious freedom, many more saw the vast untamed land and its bounty of untapped resources as an opportunity to make money. In 1609, the Dutch East India Company, the first big company to trade goods throughout Europe and Asia, hired the explorer Henry Hudson to find a northwest passage from Holland to India through the frozen Arctic. Today the passage is navigable, but then it was blocked by ice, so Hudson failed his mission. However, he did succeed in claiming the lands on either side of what is now the Hudson River for the Dutch. He named it New Netherland, and the region that is now Manhattan he named New Amsterdam. Dutch settlers moved in quickly. There they discovered plentiful wildlife such as beavers, otter, mink, and fox, whose pelts could be used for fur, which was in great demand among Europeans back home. Suppliers made a lot of money, and New Amsterdam quickly became an important fur-trading port.

Although the settlement thrived, Dutch dominance in North America was short-lived. At this time, the early seventeenth century, England and Holland were the wealthiest and most powerful nations in Europe. When the British saw how profitable the Dutch settlement was, the English decided to fight for rule. In 1664, the British navy overpowered the unpopular colonial governor, Peter Stuyvesant. The colony that was New Netherland was renamed New York, in honor of the king's brother, James, Duke of York, who had strategized the takeover. Despite the transition of rule, the Dutch settlers remained and lived among the new British settlers in continued peace and **prosperity**.

Those with the financial means paid their own passage, and those who could not often came through the system of indentured servitude, whereby wealthy patrons and landowners paid their fare. In return for their paid travel expenses and their room and board upon arrival, these **indentured servants** would be required to work for the patron, or master, for the length of their indenture—an agreed-upon amount of time (typically five to seven years). Upon completion of this contract, the indentured servant was no longer required to work for the patron.

Checkpoint

✓ Checkpoint

Read More About It

Go to your local library or online to learn about the Dutch, French, and Spanish colonies in North America.

▼ The Dutch were skilled mapmakers. Their detailed sketches are still used by archaeologists today.

The Moving Frontier

As growing numbers of Europeans settled the Americas, they displaced more and more of the Native American peoples who had been there for centuries. The agreements between the European settlers and Native Americans varied from colony to colony, and though some tribal groups and settlers were able to make peace, in most cases there were regular disputes over territory and resources. Some Native American tribes and settlers learned to cooperate, while others continued to mistreat one another.

The majority of Europeans flooding into America settled near the coastline of the Atlantic Ocean. The British built cities close to the rivers of New England and the Middle Atlantic colonies, or villages on the rich farmland of the southern colonies. But as the Eastern Seaboard grew more crowded, there were also individuals who pushed the **frontier**, which bordered the territories west of the British colonies, farther and farther west. Trading posts opened, and small towns sprang up around these posts as more and more people needed supplies and services. Settling the frontier was a risky business. Clearing the land to erect homes, businesses, and schools was back-breaking work, and there was no guarantee of success. There was no guarantee of peace, either. Native Americans who had inhabited these lands for centuries were not willing to give up their home without a fight. Battles between the Native Americans and the settlers were brutal and bloody.

The French and Indian War (1754–1763)

In 1700 the population of the American colonies was about 250,000. By 1750 the British colonies had nearly 1.5 million inhabitants. Unlike the Spanish and French colonies, the British colonies were open to people of any country, and these colonists began encroaching on non-British territories. In 1754, fighting broke out between the Virginia militia and French troops along the hotly contested border between their colonies. What followed was the French and Indian War, in which the British fought the French and those Native American tribes allied with the French for dominance in North America. During this time, the colonial militias learned how to work together with the British forces to defeat a common enemy. This war was a significant training ground for many who would take up arms against their king a decade later. The bloody conflict ended in 1763, with a victorious Britain having doubled its land holdings in North America. However, the price of victory was high. It was time, England believed, for the colonies to make sacrifices for the good of the mother country.

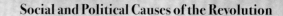

◀ The bows and arrows of Native Americans were often no match for the rifles and guns of the pioneers.

THEY MADE A DIFFERENCE

George Washington (1732–1799)

George Washington began his military career in the Virginia militia and is believed to have fired one of the first shots of the French and Indian War. His experience and training during that war helped shape the man into the military strategist he would become, giving him the skills to lead, fight, and win the American Revolution (1775–1783).

▲ France and Britain published different maps of their holdings and land claims in North America.

13

Colonial Defiance

Laws such as the Sugar Act of 1764, which put a tax on sugar, and the Quartering Act and Stamp Act of 1765 were the first of many handed down by the British crown and Parliament that were poorly received. The Quartering Act forced colonists to house British soldiers in their own homes. The Stamp Act placed a tax on all printed papers, legal documents, licenses, newspapers, and other publications, and even playing cards. While the cost of the tax was relatively small, the principle of taxing the people to raise money without their consent was viewed as unjust.

Loyalists, who accepted the burden of the new laws and taxes and were less passionate about the need for representation in government, remained true to the king and Parliament. They wanted to remain safe as subjects of the British Empire. However, many colonists did not view themselves as typical British subjects. The American colonists had been active in their own governance for more than a century and had helped fight and win the French and Indian War. Colonists had already made sacrifices and were not inclined to allow a distant king and Parliament to impose laws and mandates without their consent. They also felt the presence of such a large military force during peacetime was unnecessary.

Those who opposed the crown became known as **Patriots** and began speaking out in defiance, writing pamphlets and organizing boycotts and embargoes. These acts of treason could result in harsh punishment, but those who sought change continued to speak and act out in rebellion.

The Sons of Liberty were a rebel organization started in Boston by a group of shopkeepers and artisans known as the Loyal Nine. The group of activists protested the Stamp Act and other such acts that would follow.

Anti–Stamp Act cartoons and rhetoric warning against use of the stamps were printed in newspapers and handbills. ▶

Soon chapters of the Sons of Liberty were established in every colony—all seeking to force stamp distributors and tax collectors out of office. Though these rebels sometimes used violence, their most effective weapon in bringing about change was words. They wrote and distributed political cartoons, opinion pamphlets, and newspaper editorials to educate colonists about their cause and to bring about change.

Discontent with the Stamp Act of 1765, which was to be used to pay for 10,000 troops along the Appalachian Frontier, led to its repeal in 1766. ▼

HISTORICAL PERSPECTIVE

Mercy Otis Warren (1728–1814)

Today women have positions of power in the political arena, but in the 1770s, it was rare to find a female among the cigar-smoking, tough-talking Founders. Enter Mercy Otis. She had no formal education but had been raised in a family that believed in freedom and was willing to fight for it.

Otis married James Warren, a well-known politician. It soon became clear that she was a better speechwriter than he was. She began writing books, speeches, and articles. Many of them were published anonymously, since she was a woman and writing what would be considered traitorous words against England. A strong believer in democracy, she wrote, "The happiness of mankind depends much on the modes of government."

▲ This teapot, ironically made in England, is a celebration of the repeal of the Stamp Act.

In 1770, unarmed colonists in Boston were shot dead by British troops after hurling some snowballs at the troops. The tragedy became known as the Boston Massacre. It sent further shock waves through the colonies, solidifying a disdain for the British troops that had brought harm to the colonists, a distrust of the king, and the need for change. By 1774, when the so-called Intolerable Acts closed the port of Boston and rewrote the Massachusetts charter, installing a military government, unrest in the colonies had reached a boiling point.

On September 5, 1774, delegates from every colony met in Philadelphia, Pennsylvania, at the First Continental Congress. There they wrote to King

{ **The Root of the Meaning:** }

revolution

comes from the Latin word *revolvere*, meaning "to turn." A revolution is a complete turn toward a new kind of future, and a turn away from the past.

George III to try to find a peaceful compromise. However, King George would not negotiate and said that they must either "submit or triumph." Fighting would break out by the spring of 1775, and the Continental Congress would issue its Declaration of Independence in July 1776. For these colonists, submission was not a viable option, but **revolution** proved to be.

Summing Up

- The British colonies were settled by colonists in search of religious freedom, tolerance, and new opportunities for wealth and prosperity.

- They settled along the Eastern Seaboard and established separate governments under British rule, but they largely governed themselves from day to day.

- The colonies encountered hardships and competed for land and other resources with one another and the Native Americans who already lived there.

- After the French and Indian War, England finally began enforcing trade laws in the colonies, and resentment toward British tyranny eventually became a cry for battle.

Putting It All Together

Choose one of the following research activities. Work independently, in pairs, or in small groups. Share what you've learned with your class, and listen as others present their findings.

1 Draw a map of the American colonies in 1775. Label each colony. Research the origins of the people who settled each of the colonies and the type of colonial government they established, and define the characteristics of these governments.

2 Imagine you were a delegate at the First Continental Congress. Write an argument for the cause you are representing.

3 Visit your local library or go online to find information about the people who helped build your city and state. What Native American tribes first inhabited your region? Who were the settlers who later established communities in your area? What immigrant groups brought their customs and cultures to the place you call home? Write an essay or lecture or create a graphic poster that explains the lasting influences of these different groups.

Economic Causes of the Revolution

The ports of New England kept trading ships busy, and the mills cranked out textiles.

What economic factors led the colonies to seek self-rule?

Each colony grew or manufactured certain goods. In the South those were rice, tobacco, and, eventually, cotton. In the North there were fisheries, fur-trading posts, and forests. England's vested interests in the colonies were primarily financial, and they had come to rely on the wealth of resources as well as the money certain cash crops could generate.

Mercantilism

England kept a tight rein on the colonies through the use of **mercantilism**, an economic system popular in the 1600s and 1700s. The central tenet of mercantilism was that the colonies existed for the benefit of the colonial power. Mercantilism meant that any trade, with any foreign nation, was required to be under tight government control. It also meant that the government in power—in this case, England—could demand *exclusivity* in trade. The colonies were basically allowed to do business only with England. American colonies were forbidden to trade with any other country without special permission. In instances when England did allow it, the colonists were forced to pay hefty **tariffs**, or taxes on goods they imported from other nations.

The colonists paid, but grudgingly. Many wrote letters to newspapers protesting these unfair regulations, the steep taxes, and the restrictions this put on the money colonists could earn.

The Middle Passage

Africa to America to Europe

In colonial times, enslaved Africans were considered property and they were a valuable commodity. Enslaved people were procured by imprisonment, to be shipped, sold, and traded to fulfill certain market needs. The free labor enslaved people provided to their owners was in high demand, and the enslaved men and women were moved between continents through a system called the Triangle Trade.

Ships filled with manufactured goods departed from Europe, bound for Africa. There the goods were traded for African slaves, many of whom were kidnapped by their own countrymen. Hundreds were chained inside the ship with little food and water, and no light. The enslaved captives were then shipped across the Atlantic to North America to be sold for high profits or traded for raw materials. Those materials would go back to England, a country with the capability to convert raw materials into manufactured goods. Then the pattern began all over again. The slaves themselves were in the "Middle Passage," the voyage between continents.

PRIMARY SOURCE

Autobiography of a Slave

A slave named Olaudah Equiano related his experience of the Middle Passage in his autobiography *The Interesting Narrative of the Life of Olaudah Equiano*. He described the ship:

"The closeness of the place, and the heat of the climate, added to the number in the ship, which was so crowded that each had scarcely room to turn himself, almost suffocated us."

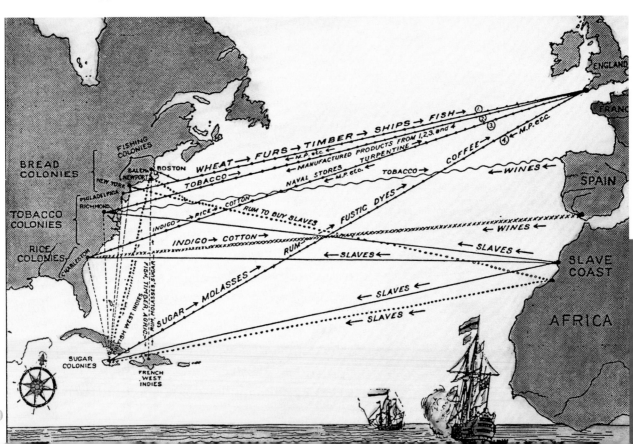

The New England Economy

New England had a bustling economy during the colonial period. It was a major source of timber. For many years, exporting timber was a profitable way for many New Englanders to make a living. Timber was also used for building homes and, eventually, boats for fishing and ships to export to other countries. New England also served as an important trading post in those years.

The period just prior to the American Revolution was the beginning of the First Industrial Revolution in Europe. Factories were springing up in New England cities. Wool from the South was brought up North and woven into cloth in textile mills.

New England felt the pressure of Britain's mercantilism. Colonists sought new markets to buy their manufactured products as well as bread, flour, pork, and other foods harvested from the rich soil of North America.

They began trading with the West Indies, another English colony, where they purchased rich molasses, sugar, and **indigo** blue dye for clothing. England didn't mind. Its government simply imposed even higher taxes.

◄ The three points of the triangle were England, Africa, and the North American colonies.

England also added to the inequities imposed by mercantilism. It instituted a system of unfavorable trade balance. This meant that the colonists had to buy more from England than England had to buy from them. The new regulations did not go over well.

Life in the Mid-Atlantic

Flour, grains, and livestock were the life's blood of the Mid-Atlantic colonies. The rich soil of Pennsylvania, New Jersey, upstate New York, Delaware, and Maryland provided a bounty of foodstuffs, which could be exported to Europe and the West Indies.

The thickly wooded forests found in these colonies provided abundant natural resources that could be used for fuel, paper, and building supplies. A good deal of commerce therefore depended on the sawmills, gristmills, and textile mills, as well as printing, publishing, and papermaking. The amount of lumber also attracted shipbuilding companies. These factors supported the steady growth of healthy industry in the region.

The combination of natural resources allowed for a variety of salable goods. And the region's broad, navigable rivers made transporting those goods a relatively smooth process. Therefore, port cities like New York and Philadelphia were both centers of government for the colonies and centers of trade and business.

Plantations and Enslaved People

Life in the southern colonies was shaped by the Plantation Economy. A plantation is a large estate in which crops such as cotton, coffee, sugar, rice, and tobacco are grown. Sometime during the 1800s, the word *plantation* came to refer to the homes where wealthy landowners lived in grand style. That has long been the stereotype. However, a closer look at history proves that is not necessarily the case. There were many plantation-style farms in the South, but there were few wealthy plantation owners. Most were simple farmers. Still, even they relied on slaves to harvest their crops.

The South

For the southern colonies—Virginia, Georgia, and North and South Carolina—life seemed to move slowly. The land was lush and green, and the temperature soared in summertime. While farmers in New England struggled to till the rocky soil, southern farmers found rich, red clay that held the moisture that also hung in the humid air. Here the economy rested solidly on rice and tobacco, and later cotton. The harvesting of these crops was performed by enslaved labor.

In order to grow enough rice and tobacco, southern farmers, who lived on **plantations**, needed hundreds of hands to raise the rice and pick the tobacco leaves. Growing these crops on a small piece of land would not bring in enough money for a family to survive, but huge-scale planting would help the South grow rich. Enslaved labor became a crucial part of the South's survival. Because the enslaved laborers would not receive a wage, all profits would go directly to the plantation owner.

◄ The southern colonies relied on enslaved labor to help harvest massive amounts of rice, tobacco, and later cotton.

▲ Many Native American tribes wanted the English to win the Revolutionary War in the hopes that white settlers would stop plundering their lands.

The Iroquois Nation

Five Native American tribes—the Mohawk, Oneida, Onondaga, Cayuga, and Seneca—joined together to form an alliance. Calling themselves the Iroquois Nation, they had several goals.

Most important, they fought to protect themselves and the lands they inhabited, which stretched from New York State all the way up to Ontario, Canada.

They also hoped to succeed in commerce, the buying and selling of goods and services, with the newly arrived settlers from Europe.

Unlike most Native American tribes, they sided with Britain in what is called the French and Indian War, in which France and England fought over American colonial territory from 1754 to 1763. While most Native American tribes, having been treated unfairly by the British, sided with the French, the Iroquois Nation made a different decision. They believed that if Great Britain were to win the war, it would honor its friendship with the Iroquois and guarantee them land grants—something France was not prepared to do.

Then the American Revolution broke out. Most of the tribes remained loyal to Britain, but the Oneida broke away to side with the colonists. When the Americans won the war, General George Washington ordered that the tribes on the side of the English be destroyed. The few surviving Iroquois moved farther up into Canada. Later wars eventually led to the removal and transfer of all Native Americans to reservations.

Intolerable Acts

Mill operators in New England, farmers in New Jersey, and rice plantation owners in South Carolina were all being hit hard by 1774 for the same reason. The Navigation Acts, which collected taxes and raised money for England, suddenly became a symbol for tyranny and **oppression** in the eyes of the colonists.

Since the 1650s, when colonists began building their homes in America, England had demanded high taxes and tariffs on British goods shipped to the colonies. The monies collected were to help finance Great Britain's far-flung empire. Since the majority of colonists considered themselves loyal British subjects, they accepted these taxes.

By the 1770s, however, the taxes became a real strain on the colonists' ability to eke out a profit. At the very least, it was argued, the colonists should have a say in the amount they would pay. Additionally, as long as they were under British rule, it made sense that they should have proper representation in the Houses of Parliament, the lawmaking body of government. The British did not see it that way. They believed the colonists were unreasonable, and worse, they labeled those who questioned their authority outright traitors. The British government passed a series of laws, known as the Navigation Acts, to tighten the reins on their subjects. Each law, or act, levied a new tax—or form of punishment. Colonists who had patriotically paid their taxes were

▲ The Boston Tea Party

suddenly made to feel like criminals for suggesting that their money should guarantee them a say in government.

"No taxation without representation" became the colonial battle cry. The first object of their wrath was tea.

For years, colonial merchants had been smuggling in low-quality tea without paying any tax. In December 1773, tons of high-quality tea leaves were shipped to Boston Harbor in Massachusetts to be imported at a lower tax rate which could compete with the smuggled "tax-free" tea. When news of the tea spread, many ports let the tea rot on their docks. One evening the Boston merchants decided to go one step further and protest. Many of these protesters had, that very evening, attended a town meeting led by Samuel Adams, who urged them to revolt. The protesters then donned disguises and pretended to be members of the Mohawk Indian tribe—a tribe that inspired fear among the English, due to their raids against colonial forts. Every crate of tea was dumped into the sea. This became known as the Boston Tea Party. When word got to King George III, he was irate and decided to punish anyone involved.

Acts of Parliament 1763–1774

Name	Year	Intended Purpose	Result
Sugar Act	1764	to raise money to pay for soldiers in North America	The British government forced the colonists to pay duties on the molasses and sugar it received from such British colonies as the West Indies.
Currency Act	1764	Colonists wanted permission to print their own paper money.	The British government said no, that only British paper money could be used.
Stamp Act	1765	to raise money to pay for England's soldiers	This act required colonists to purchase special watermarked (or "stamped") paper for everything from legal documents to newspapers.
Quartering Act	1765	British troops living in the colonies needed places to live and food to eat.	The British government ruled that any unoccupied private home could be commandeered by troop leaders to use as a barracks. American colonists would pay a tax to help shelter and feed a certain number of soldiers.
Declaratory Act	1766	to punish protests and boycotts by colonists	The Stamp Act was repealed—a colonist victory—but this act declared that Britain had the right to issue any kind of tax it wanted.
Tea Act	1773	To raise money for England. The Tea Act lowered taxes on any tea shipped to the British colonies from the East India Tea Company, in order to undercut profits and compete with lower-priced smuggled tea.	the Boston Tea Party and other protests
Intolerable Acts	1774	Retribution for the colonists' continued rebellion against the British Crown. These acts gave English courts the power to rule over legal matters in the colonies and select governing officials. The acts also closed down all Boston ports.	the Revolutionary War

Fighting the French

Throughout recorded history, England and France, close neighbors on the map, fought each other for power and prestige. Both countries were trying to build **imperial** power in Europe. In 1754 these rivals fought on American soil, where both ruled territories, in the French and Indian War. Most Native Americans supported the French in their battles with the British.

By the 1750s France had colonies in Canada as well as territories in Louisiana and along the Mississippi River, with just over 75,000 French colonists. The British boasted over 1.5 million colonists, inhabiting the land stretching from what is now Georgia up to Canada's Newfoundland.

It was inevitable the two nations would argue, and they did—over everything from who ran which fort to who should be allowed to explore new territories. The French **brokered,** or negotiated, an alliance with several Native American tribes, and together they battled the vast British army and colonists. In the end, however, France could not match England's might.

HISTORICAL PERSPECTIVE

The Sun Never Sets on the British Empire

"The sun never sets on the British Empire" was an expression made popular in the 1820s, but it was just as applicable in the 1700s. It meant that the English monarchy had dominion around the globe. The colonies—whether they were in the Americas, Africa, or Asia—were a critical part of Britain's economy and were also useful as strategic spots for military bases and trading ports.

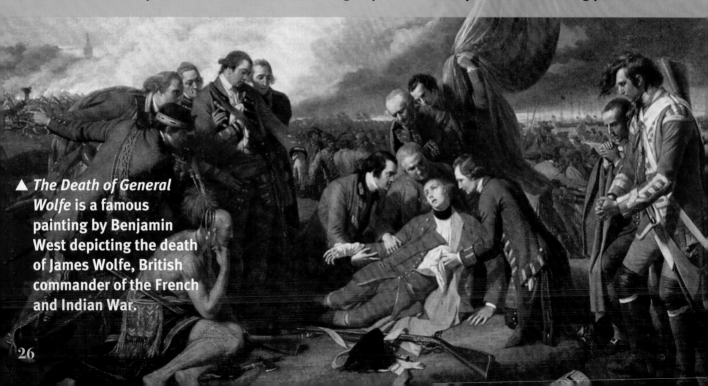

▲ *The Death of General Wolfe* is a famous painting by Benjamin West depicting the death of James Wolfe, British commander of the French and Indian War.

George Washington Fights for England

Fort Duquesne, a French post located along the Ohio River, was considered an important military camp for France. An incident in 1753 involving the fort marked the first appearance of the man who would one day lead the way to freedom in the Revolutionary War.

The British-appointed lieutenant governor of the Virginia Colony, Robert Dinwiddie, grew concerned about the presence of the French at the fort. He sent a twenty-two-year-old Virginia militia officer to the fort to inform the French that they were trespassing on Virginia's territory, and also to assess their strengths. This was the first important job for the young officer, whose name was George Washington, a surveyor who would later be thrust into history. When the French refused to meet with Washington, a battled ensued. The Virginia militia successfully sacked the fort but was soon beaten back. This skirmish was the first battle of the French and Indian War.

PRIMARY SOURCE

The Journal of George Washington

George Washington kept detailed notes of his trip to ask the French to leave their post. Those notes became a journal, first published as a pamphlet in Williamsburg, Virginia. Later, it was reproduced in two installments of the *Maryland Gazette*. It is considered one of the most important documents in American history.

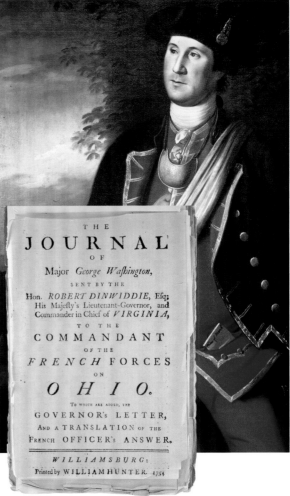

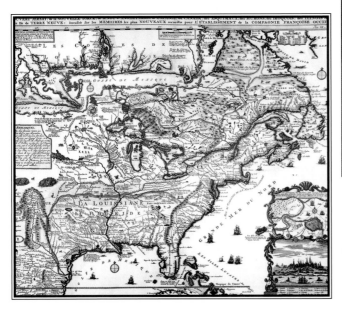

◀ This map shows the French territory in the seventeenth century, then called New France.

The Spoils of War

The French and Indian War raged from 1754 until 1763. Thousands of lives were lost. This war went down in history as the very first global conflict. Battles were fought in every British and French colony, on the seas and on land.

The result of this conflict would have major repercussions for America. England's victory gave it status as the greatest colonial power in the world, with control of North America and India. But the war would leave England nearly bankrupt. England had exhausted its resources and put itself in great debt defending its stake in the colonies. For the crown to recoup its financial losses, while financing the defense of its new territories, it would have to impose heavy taxes on the colonies and start enforcing the many trade laws it had ignored for more than a century. It was the cost of the war that led England to raise its taxes on the colonies. For almost 100 years, the British had failed to enforce the Navigation Acts. Three thousand miles of ocean lay between England and the colonies, and with England distracted by its own wars on the European continent, it had allowed the colonists to make many local decisions themselves without consulting the British authorities.

To keep the peace with Native Americans, the Proclamation of 1763 restricted British settlement west of the Appalachian Mountains. This law angered colonists who wanted

▲ The Proclamation of 1763, which banned further migration west of the Appalachians, increased tension between colonists and the crown.

to move west and take advantage of those lands and their abundant resources. Enforcement of the long-ignored Navigation Acts also left the colonists angry and powerless, with no representation in Parliament. New tax laws passed by England further enraged the colonists, inciting rebellion and the opening acts of the Revolutionary War.

Summing Up

- England benefited greatly from its colonies, charged high taxes on its goods, and limited the colonies' trade with other nations.

- The French and Indian War, and the pressure it put on England to raise money, was the leading economic cause of the American Revolution.

- The high tariffs and strict regulations without any colonial representative voice in British Parliament led to acts of rebellion and the popular slogan "No Taxation Without Representation."

Putting It All Together

Choose one of the following research activities. Work independently, in pairs, or in small groups. Share what you've learned with your class, and listen as others present their findings.

1 Use a blank map of the American colonies and fill in the names of each colony. Review what goods and services were provided by each colony. Make a key that represents goods and resources for each region.

2 Pretend you work for a newspaper during colonial times. Write an editorial where you explain your response to one of the acts of Parliament between 1763 and 1774.

3 Choose one of the Intolerable Acts. Which do you think was the hardest on the colonists? Why?

✓ Checkpoint

Think About It

How are the results of the French and Indian War connected to the Acts of Parliament from 1763 to 1774?

CARTOONIST'S NOTEBOOK
ILLUSTRATED BY GARY FREEMAN

YOU'VE NEVER FAILED ME BEFORE, THOMPSON!

YOUR SHIPMENT WILL BE IN THURSDAY NEXT, MR. PRESCOTT.

LET'S HOPE ALL THIS NONSENSE WITH THE CROWN AND THE REBEL MOB IS SETTLED SOON, SO WE CAN GET BACK TO BUSINESS!

AYE! GOOD DAY AND GOD SAVE THE KING.

WHAT'S THE MEANING OF THIS, ADAMS?

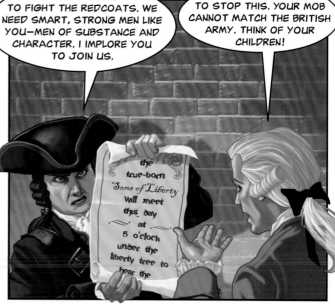

WE ARE GOING TO FIGHT THE REDCOATS. WE NEED SMART, STRONG MEN LIKE YOU—MEN OF SUBSTANCE AND CHARACTER. I IMPLORE YOU TO JOIN US.

I IMPLORE YOU TO STOP THIS. YOUR MOB CANNOT MATCH THE BRITISH ARMY. THINK OF YOUR CHILDREN!

SHOULD JOHN THOMPSON JOIN THE REBEL FORCES? YES OR NO? SUPPORT YOUR ARGUMENT WITH FACTS FROM THE TEXT.

Ideological Causes of the War

In the mid-1700s, the introduction of a new, powerful series of ideas inspired people to believe they had a right to independence. *Intellect* means "the capacity for knowledge." *Intellectual* means "thinking logically and making use of ideas."

◀ Ben Franklin began his career as a printer.

What were the new ideas influencing people's thoughts about their right to independence?

The Age of Enlightenment

To *enlighten* means "to inform or instruct, to find out something not previously known or considered." Think of enlightenment as a "lightbulb" that goes off in your head, symbolizing an exciting idea or solution to a problem.

During what we now call the Age of Enlightenment, **philosophers** in Europe and the Americas wrote articles, essays, and pamphlets about the importance of democracy, liberty, and freedom from oppression. They put forth the notion that believing in science and reason made more sense than simply believing that the monarchy and church were always right. In other words, science could be used to make the world a better place, and human beings could be in control of their own destiny (rather than relying on religious "higher powers").

For example, in the past, if a government was oppressive, people believed that it was the will of God, since monarchs were thought to be endowed with divine authority. With the advent of ideas from the **Enlightenment**, such as the power of the individual, suddenly people understood that they had the right to oppose an oppressive government. Or that poverty and ignorance are not the will of God, but conditions that could be changed by using science to create a social plan to better people's lives.

Although revolutionary at the time, these concepts weren't new. The principles of freedom and democracy were as old as ancient Greece and Rome.

HISTORY AND TECHNOLOGY

Although the printing press had been in use since the 1400s, advances in technology by the 1700s had made printing easier and cheaper. As a result, publications became available to anyone who cared to read them. Colonists were receiving their news from newspapers and pamphlets. This marked a huge change in society. Now everyone in a community, not just an elite group of wealthy individuals, could learn what was happening locally and all over the world. That is primarily how the ideas of the Enlightenment reached them.

Ancient Greece

In the ancient city of Athens, citizens founded the first democracy, which means "rule by the people." And in theory, that is how leaders were chosen. In reality in those days, only wealthy white men could vote in Athens. However, everyone from the poorest peasants to laborers to women had the right to air their opinions. The Parthenon—the most famous structure in Greece—was a temple, but also a place where people gathered to be heard.

Ancient Rome

In the Roman Republic, citizens did not trust any one person to have total power over the people. They did not want Rome to be led by a **dictator**. To avoid this, leaders broke government into three components: an executive branch, a legislative branch, and a judicial branch. Each branch kept an eye on the others to make sure none had too much power. Today the United States government also has three branches in order to maintain a balance of power.

Europe's Age of Enlightenment

John Locke (1632–1704)

Born in England to Puritan parents, John Locke was educated at Oxford University and became a well-known doctor. After he saved the life of the first Earl of Shaftesbury, who had been suffering from a liver infection, Locke entered the world of politics and wealth. However, he always remembered the message his parents had instilled in him—that liberty was the most important ideal of all. His dedication to the beliefs of liberty, free will, reason, tolerance, and separation of church and state, and in a binding contract between a government and its subjects, made him a true advocate of the common person. His writings influenced the great French and Scottish philosophers as well as the American revolutionaries.

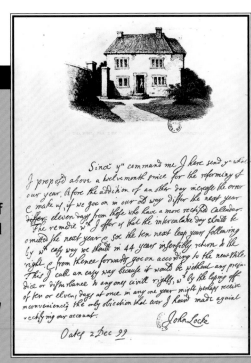

PRIMARY SOURCE

Locke's *Second Treatise of Government*

John Locke's massive written work *The Second Treatise of Government* had an enormous effect on the people who would soon declare their independence from Great Britain. In the section he called "On Tyranny," Locke spoke about the evils of oppression and the denial of rights. He was greatly influenced on these subjects by Isaac Newton, a scholar during the Age of Enlightenment known as the father of science. "A government is not free to do what it pleases . . . the law of nature, as revealed by Newton, stands as an eternal rule to all men . . . tyranny is the exercise of power beyond right, which no body can have a right to."

John Locke

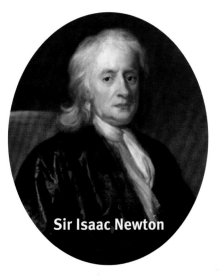

Sir Isaac Newton

Mary Wollstonecraft

Sir Isaac Newton (1642–1727)

Sir Isaac Newton was an English physicist and mathematician who was one of the most influential scientists of all time and a key figure in the scientific revolution. He invented calculus, and his writings and discoveries laid the foundation for much of what we know today about physics, including the laws of motion and gravity, and Earth's place in the universe. In the 1690s, he also began investigating the Bible and questioning religion.

Mary Wollstonecraft (1759–1797)

Mary Wollstonecraft was a British writer, philosopher, and early advocate of women's rights who lived during the latter half of the eighteenth century. Wollstonecraft's work was a major influence on many women in the Western world. Wollstonecraft is most famous for writing *A Vindication of the Rights of Woman* (1792), in which she argued that women are not inferior to men by nature but by lack of education. She urged women to be more than just wives and caretakers: women should educate children and act as companions to their husbands, not as subservient members of the household. Her writing fueled much controversy but made a lasting impression on both women and men in the years to come.

Together, along with French and Scottish philosophers, these great theorists of Europe proposed a new set of ideals for people to think about.

✓

Checkpoint

Think About It

What do terms like *rights*, *freedom*, and *liberty* mean to you?

America's Brightest

The Age of Enlightenment started in Europe, but American colonists boasted many brilliant thinkers as well.

Thomas Jefferson (1743–1826)

Writer, inventor, politician—Thomas Jefferson was a man of many talents. The third of ten children born to Jane Randolph and Peter Jefferson of Virginia, Thomas was always curious and very, very smart. He studied Latin, Greek, and French at school, but he was also fascinated with nature. He attended the College of William and Mary in Virginia, studied law and languages, and became a devoted student of music, playing classical and folk music on his violin.

While Jefferson was in college, one of his professors, William Small, introduced him to the ideas of the Enlightenment. For Jefferson, those ideas went beyond the basics of liberty and freedom from tyranny. From enlightened thinkers he developed a belief in the strength of the common man and the nobility of nature and the land. He believed that people who lived closest to nature were those who knew the truest freedom.

Thomas Jefferson became involved in Virginia politics and served as a delegate to the Second Continental Congress. As talk of independence and revolution spread around Philadelphia, Jefferson,

Although a group of men is credited with drafting the Declaration of Independence, it is believed that Thomas Jefferson was the main author of the document. ▶

PRIMARY SOURCE

A Letter from Thomas Jefferson

"Enlighten the people, generally, and tyranny of expressions and body and mind will vanish like spirits at the dawn of day."

(1816 letter to his friend, French economist Pierre Samuel du Pont de Nemours)

along with friend Benjamin Franklin and sometime-rival John Adams, found himself on a committee to draft a statement that would declare America's independence from England.

Thomas Jefferson would hold many offices throughout his lifetime—governor of Virginia, secretary of state for George Washington, vice president to John Adams, and ambassador to France—before he was elected America's third president in 1801.

Benjamin Franklin (1706–1790)

Benjamin Franklin was an innovative American thinker, publisher, diplomat, scientist, and inventor. More than any other Founding Father, he traveled frequently between the American colonies and Europe during the Enlightenment. He helped exchange ideas between nations and had a profound influence on the formation of the new government of the United States. Franklin had a hand in both the Declaration of Independence and the U.S. Constitution.

The Native American Influence

Whether colonists and neighboring tribes respected or feared one another, as time wore on they needed one another as trading partners, allies, and sources of land, goods, labor, and other resources. They also shared ideas, and the Native American system of governance has proven to have profoundly influenced the Europeans who settled North America.

The shining example is the Iroquois Confederacy, a union of tribes running the extent of the Eastern Seaboard. The confederacy had a firmly established democratic government in place before the first European explorers landed in North America. The Iroquois Constitution of the Five Nations, also known as the Great Law of Peace, outlines this government and was used as a touchstone for those who would later seek independence and write the United States Constitution.

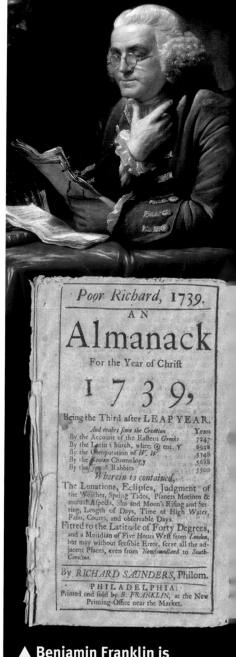

▲ Benjamin Franklin is remembered for many things, among them a publication called *Poor Richard's Almanack*. "A penny saved is a penny earned," one of his most famous quotes, was first printed in it.

◄ According to legend, Dekanawida (seated) helped establish the Iroquois Great Law, which later served as a guide for the framers of the United States Constitution.

Independence Is Declared!

England's unfair treatment of the colonists and the new ideas of the Age of Enlightenment were on a collision course. When the settlers asked for reforms, England said no. When they asked for fair representation in British government and relief from taxes, they were turned down. When they wanted to trade with other nations that were not part of the British Empire, they were told no. The stage was set for the American Revolution.

On July 4, 1776, when the Second Continental Congress read Thomas Jefferson's Declaration into public record, every colonist knew that its message would be a warning shot to Great Britain's King George III.

HISTORICAL PERSPECTIVE

Freedom for All?

George Washington, Thomas Jefferson, and many other Founding Fathers supported freedom for all, but they also owned enslaved people. Although in his heart Jefferson knew that slavery was, as he put it, "an abominable crime," he did not mention independence for slaves in his Declaration. He knew if he said anything negative about slavery, the other southern delegates would never sign the Declaration of Independence.

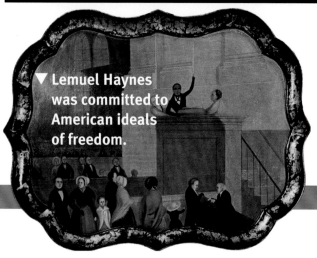

▼ Lemuel Haynes was committed to American ideals of freedom.

THEY MADE A DIFFERENCE

LEMUEL HAYNES (1753–1833)

When the men who wrote the Declaration of Independence dipped their quill pens into inkwells to sign the agreement that "all men are created equal," they weren't really talking about "all men." White, land-owning, business-running men were created equal. The same did not hold true for the enslaved Africans brought to American shores in chains.

Lemuel Haynes was an indentured servant in Massachusetts—not technically a slave but in many ways living like one. The key difference was that an indentured servant was required by law to be educated. Haynes was one of the few African American men of the period who could read and write.

Despite his own lack of real freedom, Haynes fought for the rights of others when he joined the Revolutionary Army. After the war, he wrote many pamphlets to spread his message: "Liberty is equally as precious to a black man, as it is to a white one, and bondage is equally as intolerable to the one as it is to the other."

PRIMARY SOURCE

The Declaration of Independence, 1776
(EXCERPT)

When, in the course of human events, it becomes necessary for one people to dissolve the political bands which have connected them with another, and to assume among the powers of the earth, the separate and equal station to which the laws of nature and of nature's God entitle them, a decent respect to the opinions of mankind requires that they should declare the causes which impel them to the separation.

We hold these truths to be self-evident, that all men are created equal, that they are endowed by their Creator with certain unalienable rights, that among these are life, liberty and the pursuit of happiness . . .

Thomas Paine's *Common Sense*

While the Declaration of Independence was making news, another document from another man named Thomas was giving colonists a huge jolt of *Common Sense*.

In his native England, Thomas Paine worked for the British government as a goods inspector. He got fired. He also worked as a British schoolteacher. He got fired. He opened a tobacco shop. It failed. He was almost sent to debtor's prison, but instead was given permission to move to the American colonies. There he began a new life as a journalist and newspaperman who, not surprisingly, had little love for his native country.

In January 1776, Paine wrote *Common Sense*, a pamphlet that urged separation from England and full-on war against oppression. To avoid being jailed as a traitor, he published his work **anonymously** so that no one would know who wrote it. It was a huge seller and is widely credited with swaying mass opinion toward independence.

HISTORY AND LITERATURE

Common Sense

Thomas Paine's *Common Sense* fueled the fires of revolution by challenging England's right to power and demanding that oppression come to an end. Paine wrote: "As a long and violent abuse of power is generally the means of calling the right of it in question and as the king of England hath undertaken in his own right to support the parliament in what he calls theirs, and as the good people of this country are grievously oppressed by the combination, they have an undoubted privilege to inquire into the pretensions of both, and equally to reject the usurpations of either."

The Crisis

(published in December 1776; it also helped rally the Patriots)

These are the times that try men's souls. The summer soldier and the sunshine patriot will, in this crisis, shrink from the service of their country; but he that stands by it now, deserves the love and thanks of man and woman. Tyranny, like hell, is not easily conquered; yet we have this consolation with us, that the harder the conflict, the more glorious the triumph. What we obtain too cheap, we esteem too lightly: it is dearness only that gives every thing its value. Heaven knows how to put a proper price upon its goods; and it would be strange indeed if so celestial an article as FREEDOM should not be highly rated.

Summing Up

- The Enlightenment was a period of great thinkers and written works that inspired the ideals of freedom and liberty.

- Men such as Thomas Jefferson and Thomas Paine used the ideals of the Enlightenment to urge the colonies to free themselves from British rule.

- The Declaration of Independence announced America's intention to fight its oppressors.

Putting It All Together

Choose one of the following research activities. Work independently, in pairs, or in small groups. Share what you've learned with your class, and listen as others present their findings.

1 Declare your independence. If you were going to start a new country, what rights would matter most to you and why?

2 Find out more about one of the figures of the enlightenment. Are there other women and minorities whose contributions have been overlooked? How did they affect history?

3 Many government buildings in Washington, D.C. were inspired by Greek and Roman architecture. View pictures of buildings such as the U.S. Capitol or the Lincoln Memorial and compare them to pictures of the Parthenon in Greece or the Colosseum in Rome. Why did the builders in Washington choose those designs? Do you think they symbolize the belief that much of American history, our values and ideals, is an extension of Western civilization?

Checkpoint

Reread

Thomas Paine's *Common Sense* was written in the flowery parlance of the day. Break it down into modern language. What do you think it means?

A Triumphant Choice

▲ The First and Second Continental Congress met in Philadelphia, Pennsylvania, and produced the Declaration of Independence in 1776. Just a few years earlier, leaders such as Benjamin Franklin had thought of themselves as loyal British citizens.

King George had laid down an ultimatum in 1773, after the Boston Tea Party: the colonists would have to submit or triumph. Within a few years, the colonists had decided to try their luck, and the rebellion was upon him. However, the colonists were not simply rising up against what they believed to be excessive taxation on the goods they traded; they were rebelling against a government that would impose a tax on people who had no fair representation in British Parliament, the government that legislated for them. They were rising up against the thousands of British troops on guard in the thirteen American colonies who seemed to defend British economic interests and not the colonists themselves. By 1775, many colonists had embraced the ideology of the Enlightenment. They had become accustomed to a degree of self-governance, being so far away from the colonial power, and begun to perceive themselves as worthy of liberty and equality, and a government that also deemed them worthy. They had helped fight and win the French and Indian War and saw themselves as entitled to their independence. They were ready for change, and many were willing to die in order to bring an end to British tyranny.

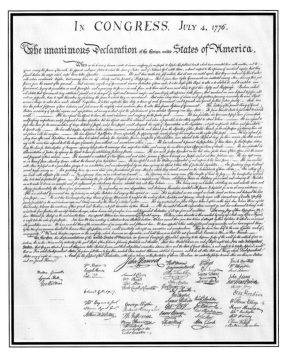

▲ **The Declaration of Independence explained why colonists had the right to be independent from England.**

▲ **The Royal British Navy had ships docked at the ports of all of its colonies. The ships' presence was a warning to the colonists: they were being watched and guarded at every moment.**

How to Write an Argument

1. Choose a topic that interests you. It should be a topic on which people have differing opinions.

2. Research the topic well. Find evidence and statistics on the topic.

3. Take a position on the topic based on your research.

4. Decide on the format and audience for your argument.

5. Outline your piece of writing.

6. Write a first draft.

   Remember a few tips:

   a. State your position and present a few strong reasons to support it.

   b. Write a clear paragraph to present each reason. Include evidence to support your position.

   c. Write a strong conclusion in which you restate your position.

7. Revise and proofread your writing. Are there presumptions in your argument that you need to support?

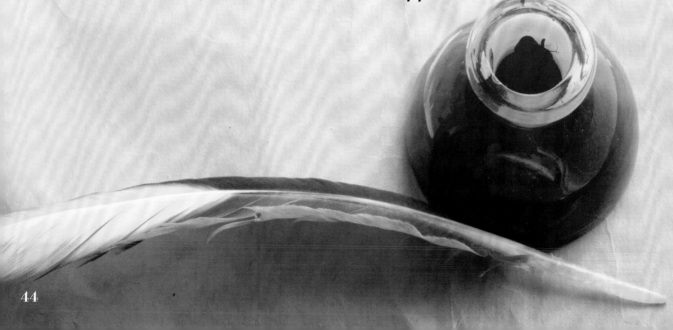

Loyalist Argument

The British colonies must remain loyal to the king. As we know all too well, a unified empire is a strong empire that benefits us all, promotes defense, and is good for trade, which is good for all. The cost of being part of a great empire is that we must follow British law and pay British taxes. Without this contract between the people and the government, our society is not sustainable and we will have nothing but chaos.

The crown came to our aid and protected us from the French and Indian groups who would have taken our lands and our livelihoods. It is our solemn duty to repay that debt and not ask for representation on the other side of the world, which would be, above all else, impractical.

Patriot Argument

People are born with certain rights—a right to live, to be free, to own land, to prosper, and even to pursue their interests. We believe in forming a government that cannot tread on these rights and that cannot take our hard-earned property by way of unlawful and unfair taxation. We must rise up against a government that would levy a tax on its people without fair representation in that government body. And since a great ocean exists between us and that government, and we do not feel that we would ever be sufficiently represented in such a Parliament, we must establish our own government, on our own land—a government of the people, by the people, and for the people. We fought alongside the redcoats for this land in the French and Indian War, and now those British troops by order of their king are turning on us. We must fight back. They have given us no other acceptable choice.

 Glossary

anonymously	(uh-NAH-nih-mus-lee) *adverb* unidentified by choice (page 40)
banishment	(BA-nish-ment) *noun* the state of being exiled or cast out of one's home country (page 10)
broker	(BROH-ker) *verb* to negotiate (page 26)
dictator	(DIK-tay-ter) *noun* a ruler with absolute power (page 34)
Enlightenment	(in-LY-ten-ment) *noun* a movement in the eighteenth century centered on the critical and scientific examination of old beliefs (page 33)
frontier	(frun-TEER) *noun* border between settled and unsettled areas (page 12)
imperial	(im-PEER-ee-ul) *adjective* relating to an empire or kingdom (page 26)
indentured servant	(in-DEN-cherd SER-vunt) *noun* someone bound to work by legal contract for a specified number of years in payment of a debt (page 11)
indigo	(IN-dih-goh) *noun* blue dye obtained from several species of the *Indigofera* plant (page 21)
Loyalist	(LOY-uh-list) *noun* a person who remained loyal to Great Britain during the American Revolution (page 14)
mercantilism	(MER-kun-ty-lih-zum) *noun* economic system in which governments strictly regulate the buying and selling of goods and create colonies to further the country's monetary wealth (page 19)
monarchy	(MAH-nar-kee) *noun* a form of government in which a sole, absolute, and royal individual rules the state or country (page 8)

oppression	(uh-PREH-shun) *noun* cruel or unjust treatment at the hands of an authority (page 24)
Patriot	(PAY-tree-ut) *noun* one who sided with the thirteen colonies during the Revolutionary War (page 14)
persecution	(per-sih-KYOO-shun) *noun* the hostile or ill treatment of a group or individual (page 8)
philosopher	(fih-LAH-suh-fer) *noun* a thinker or scholar (page 33)
Pilgrim	(PIL-grim) *noun* a religious Separatist from England who settled in Plymouth (page 8)
plantation	(plan-TAY-shun) *noun* a large farming estate usually worked by resident labor (page 22)
prosperity	(prah-SPAIR-ih-tee) *noun* a condition of thriving economically (page 11)
revolution	(reh-vuh-LOO-shun) *noun* a forced overthrow of a government in order to create a better one (page 16)
tariff	(TAIR-if) *noun* a system of taxes on imported or exported goods (page 19)
theocracy	(thee-AH-kruh-see) *noun* a government in which rulers are regarded as divinely guided (page 10)
theologian	(thee-uh-LOH-jun) *noun* a person who studies religious beliefs and practices (page 10)
tolerance	(TAH-luh-runs) *noun* peaceful coexistence of people with differing beliefs or practices (page 10)

Index